I0161019

In and Out

of Dreaming

Poems by Jay Curtis

Copyright © 2017 Jay Curtis. All
rights reserved. No portion, in part or
in the whole, of this work may be
copied, duplicated, electronically
transmitted, or otherwise distributed
in any form without the written
permission of the author.

Published in the United States of
America
Deposited in the Library of Congress

Set in Century 12 Point
Graphic Consultation: LaPointe
Illustrations
www.CatherineLaPointe.com

Cover Photograph and Front Cover
Consultation: Julia Cortese

First Edition

Lexingford Publishing LLC
New York   Hong Kong   Ottawa
San Francisco
www.lexingfordpublishingllc.com

A portion of the proceeds of each sale of this book will be sent to the ALS Association, www.alsa.org. Thank you for supporting their tireless efforts on behalf of ALS patients and their families.

What's Being Said about *In and Out of Dreaming*

"Jay's poems are amazing...sorry to use that overused word...but it is true. This collection of poems is a beautiful and insightful read. There is one poem in particular that strikes a personal cord. 'Yesterday, Today Was Tomorrow' which touches on what matters most in my work as a TV Announcer, that all important use of 'time.' The subject matter also speaks so profoundly to Jay's personal journey with ALS. Jay admits he's beginning to feel the effects of his disease, but within these pages his mind and his writings are crystal clear, sharp and wonderful."

Joe Cipriano
Network Television Announcer &
Author *Living on Air -
Adventures in Broadcasting*

"Humbling, sobering and heart wrenching, these poems embody the definition of bravery and courage which should be valued as an heirloom and passed on to anyone that is dealing with life threatening adversities."

Howard Barish
President, Kandoo Films
Producer · Documentary *13th British Academy Award Winner*

"This is a very important collection of poetry for medical trainees and providers, as well as patients."

Shanna K. Patterson, M.D.
Director of the Electromyography (EMG) Laboratory at Mount Sinai West and Mount Sinai St. Luke's Hospitals in New York City

"Jay's profound writings are infused
with both wry humor and tragedy
leaving the reader wanting
more. With humorous and
heartbreaking honesty, Jay's
reflections lift the lid on our own
souls. Masterful!"

Teri Thompson, author of *The
Power of Real-Time Social Media
Marketing: How to Attract and
Retain Customers and Grow the
Bottom Line in the Globally
Connected World* (McGraw Hill)

"I am honored to have been chosen to
read about Jay's daily physical
struggles, and my eyes overflow with
salty pools of tears celebrating Jay's
enlightening triumphs. To one
particular poem I have an answer:
I will always be near to help Jay 'Zip
Up His Coat'"

Roberta Gonzales
CBS KPIX San Francisco;
Weather Anchor/Reporter for
over 20 years

"We met at sea long ago, on an outbound ferry, when life gave us gifts it's now taking away. His poems are to me an undulant truth reflecting off those waves. It is a pleasure knowing, and now reading Jay."

Lawrence Jordan
Director/Producer

"Jay Curtis has written an elegantly blunt, hauntingly honest book of poetry. He allows us to glimpse into his world of love, pain, fear and hope as he and his family deal with the cruelty of a fatal disease. Stark and beautifully written, it is impossible to put down!"

Jeff Guidry
Author, *An Eagle Named Freedom – My True Story of a Remarkable Friendship*

Dedication

To my wife Becky and my son JT

Preface

I have been a proud member of the Writers Guild of America for decades. I spent most of my professional career as a promo writer/producer/director at CBS Television City in Hollywood. I also write poetry. I write right-handed. In 2015, I was having trouble with my fingers curling up and with weakness in my right hand and arm. On December 1, 2015, I was diagnosed with ALS (Amyotrophic Lateral Sclerosis). The condition is commonly referred to as Lou Gehrig's disease. It is the same disease that afflicts Stephen Hawking. I have asked my neurologists if I will be able to hit baseballs like Gehrig and think like Hawking. Hey, you have to laugh.

As my nervous system is compromised, muscle weakness keeps progressing. Recently it has gone to my throat and tongue. My speech is slurred and swallowing can be difficult. ALS is a fatal disease that continues to confound the medical profession, so currently there is no cure or much in the way of treatment. There is no definite death date that comes with the diagnosis, but I believe that until now, I saw my life span as infinite. That doesn't mean that I thought I would live forever, just that I didn't think much about the words THE END coming up in the credit roll of my life story. This book is about my realization that my life has become finite and that there is something inside me that is short-circuiting my essential electrical wiring. I have decided to use my creative power to chronicle my journey.

I am a poet. I'm not sure that is a title one can self-bestow. Suffice it to say that I have been writing poetry since 1970. I decided to document my ALS journey in the series of poems included in this book. I think it has become a vital part of my personal journey. These poems may help others understand that life is more precious when something imminent threatens to take it away.

Jay Curtis
New York
March, 2017

Contents

ALS Sentence   1

Picking Blueberries   2

Zip up My Coat   3

Human Sacrifice   4

Found Moment   5

Yesterday, Today Was Tomorrow   6

Fear Tears   7

Pauper Before the Queen   8

The Nerve Cell   9

Countdown   10

Make it Last   11

Infinitely Finite   12

Power Chords   13

Digital Signals   14

How to Boil a Frog   15

Slow Electrocution   16

Hand Me Down   17

Ruminating   18

Circus Lifer   19

Wire Walk   20

Mid Bridge   21

Eyes Open   22

Joyous Sky   24

Body Sand   25

90 Percent Man   26

Cut Flowers   27

Become Me   28

Concrete Shoes   29

Key Me   30

Monetized	31
Last Chosen	32
Agoraphobic	34
Idle Thoughts	36
Bully	37
Lemon Morning	39
Trained Junkie	40
Train Fly	42
Kind Lightning	44
Unfinished Romantics	45
In and Out of Dreaming	46
Rushing to Wait	47
All Kindling Aside	49
Trip	51
Borrowed Blue	52
Damn Amsterdam	53
Where Goes Knowledge	55
Life in Reverse	57
Medical Trial	59
Love Defined	60
35 Years On	63
Loss is Gain	65
Slurred Speech	67
The Verb To Be	68
Farewell Tour	69
Moonlit Sunrise	70
Lastly	71

ALS Sentence

You is understood
until I am the subject
looking for the verb, to live.
The sentence begins with an article,
A, and then there is a pause
while my motor neurons fire
sending my arm muscles flailing.
All other possibilities ruled out,
my spine is short-circuiting.
There is no way to fix me.
L shaped doctor's drop ceiling
looking down at my finite life,
neurological findings, cat scans
in which I am Poe's black cat
screaming inside a brick wall
for the allotted eight more lives,
no longer curious, rather cure-less.
SSSSS comes the hissing deadly
snake
that delivers the poison into my spine
as Iago poured pestilence into
Othello's ear.
Hazy gray buildings wait outside
reflecting glass pain beckons
in a window six floors in the air
that I realize doesn't open.
My bad hand feels her touch
as my wife holds on for dear life.

Picking Blueberries

My right hand defies my command
as a blueberry, like a desperate
escapee
evades capture by my finger police.
Suddenly weak and undisciplined
I am no longer caped Superman.
Kryptonite has entered my spine
and a tiny soft blue planet laughs
at my dying finger dexterity.
A deep breath centers my resolve,
"Got you, you little blue bastard!"
Time to pray, planet berry citizens.
There is a giant crushing machine
that will explode your juicy sea,
chew your terra firma to oblivion
because it still performs perfectly
sending you into my tunnel of doom
while I laugh with satisfaction
that some super powers remain.

Zip up My Coat

I want to run, but I am cold.
Zip up my coat for me.
My fingers are un-zipper-able,
yet, my legs can still propel me.

Hide my fatal wounds.
Zip up my coat for me.
Be James Dean with a cause,
as I lie outside Griffith Observatory.

Hold out your bullet filled hand,
and scream bloody murder
at the poison gang killers
who drew me out from under false
stars.

Look closer at my fading face,
you who zipped up my coat for me,
and left me warm and smiling
on this cobble stone street.

Human Sacrifice

I am no young virgin,
but grab hold of my hands
and tether my feet.
Toss me into the volcano.
Let the luscious lava lick me,
taking my flesh, muscle, bone.
Sear my heart.
Fry my brain.
Pompeii me and dot both "i"s.
Encrust my wasted lust.
Preserve my painful pose.
Let me cure undisturbed
for thousands of years.
Dig me up.
Crack me open.
Gather up the archeologists
to chant like castrato choirboys
over what the ages have left:
"Esto nobis praegustatum
Morits in examine."

Translation:
 Be for us a foretaste
 In the test of death.

Found Moment

I found a moment
wedged between before
and ever after
where the stopwatch
stopped.
Holding on with
whatever I had left
I convinced the universe
to give me years of light
to find the answers
Steven Hawking sought.
I avoided the black hole
that swallowed the repeated image
of Iron Lou Gehrig swinging
and crushing a baseball.
That ball did not die
rather it escaped, unfettered.
"That ball is going, going, gone!
But not forgotten."
Out, out among the star field,
I seek one single thing:
the path that never ends.
Forcing my trajectory to curve
I steer clear of asteroids,
avoiding the cataclysmic destruction
of the luckiest man in the Cosmos.

Yesterday, Today Was Tomorrow

You can find time,
you can lose time,
but you can't stop time.
You can take a timeout,
you can give a timeout,
but you can't stop time.
You can tell time,
but it never listens
because only time will tell.
You can bide your time,
but you can't kill time.
It will just go on and on
as you move forward in time.
You can never go back in time.
Time doesn't really stand still,
not even for you and me.
Time clicks a metronome
singing its signature song
with lyrics that cause flashes
of life's momentary highlights
jammed into my "life" movie.
I imagine there will be a moment
when all the white flashes congeal
only then will the final gun sound
hopefully, fired from a starter's pistol
merely signaling my overtime period.

Fear Tears

The waterworks are unpredictable
and who turns them on is a mystery.
Their timing is so often inopportune
because what they signal is hard to
say.
The hesitating, stifling and
shuddering
always come along for the ride.
I image myself conspicuously absent,
an empty seat on the train,
someone remembering me,
hopefully for a silly wise crack,
that ignites a flaming smile.
Now, talking to a dear friend,
I hold back the fear tears,
blaming silence on a bad connection.
And when we disconnect
I am crying hard among strangers
on a downtown subway car.
A kind woman asks, "What's the
matter?"
I reply, "Nothing, just life..."
Neglecting to add, "and death."

Pauper before the Queen

Humbled, to say the least,
I am bent down so low.
Fate holds my future
in her impossibly delicate hands.
She controls my fingers with her own,
as tiny strings connect us.
She dances in glass slippers,
tap, tap, tapping her way
to the center of my soul.
And when those slippers shatter,
I wander about inside my history
contemplating my favorite age.
Childhood?
Teen age?
Young man?
Middle age?
My finger, as best as it can,
points down to the concrete,
to the here and the now.

Nerve Cell

My nerve cells are out of line,
zapping destructive signals
down my unsuspecting spine,
destroying my arm muscles.
God damn the pusher man
shooting electrical twitches,
causing my bicep to slam
from the spell of three witches.
"Double, double toil and trouble;
fire burns, and my skin bubbles.
Cool it with a martyr's blood,
then, the arm is firm and good."
I am silvered in the moon's eclipse.
Diamonds appear on one foot sole.
My forearm proudly does back flips,
as I wonder where will go my soul.
Is there really a heaven or a hell?
Shall it be burial or cremation?
There are fancy caskets to sell.
I grow tired of my own lamentations.
April birth began the joyous march,
crossing from one century to the next.
New Year's Eve is cold and dark,
but I am ready as ever for the trek.

Countdown

I wanted to be an astronaut.
As I grew closer to the stars
my mind was in the capsules,
Mercury, Gemini, Apollo.
I orbited the planet Mars
floated in extra-vehicular activity,
and took that one small step - for
young man.
I shared it with our TV uncle Walter
then flew with Leary on an
Astroplane.
Youth is an unfulfilled hunter
often left empty at harvest time.
Returning to dust is inevitable.
Sputtering on a projected sojourn
cold and tired, staring down the moon,
hovering above a sea of tranquility,
landing in the imaginary wind
that holds up an American flag
that never really flew there.
Nothing blows boot impressions away.
Find my forever footprints in the lunar
dust.

Make it Last

When the evening sky
finds that glowing orange
that exists nowhere else,
please make it last.

When the Christmas tree
is finally fully decorated
and pine scent fills the room,
please make it last.

When the surf flows
touching my hot feet
cooling them perfectly,
please make it last.

When I see every face
that I have ever made smile
passing in my final moments,
please make them last.

Infinitely Finite

Like the line between BC and AD,
pre and post 9/11,
before the Beatles and after,
I live in the stunning aftermath
of my death-dealing diagnosis
when infinite life became finite.
Born in nineteen hundred and fifty,
I never thought I would see
the light of a new century.
Back then, sixty-five was so old
fitted with canes, filling nursing
homes,
and here I am having lived
not perfectly, but carefully
running for my health
stopping to take a deep breath.
In an unguarded pause
the hooded reaper
hands me a license to die.
I burn it like my 60's draft card,
pick up my feet and run
like a scared life thief.

Power Chords

Sound waves goodbye.
Someone is singing, screaming.
Power chords ignite the air
and I feel my clothes vibrating.
The snare drum is my head.
My son plays a guitar solo.
My ability to applaud is hampered.
God damn my right hand!
Its power cords are damaged.
Messages confuse the muscles
as they sputter down the line
from my broken brain nerve center.
Unable to snap my right fingers,
I am lost to the musical rhythm
partially out of Harlem's tune.
Will finds a way to soothe me.
The Immortal Bard reminds me
that music is the food of love
and that even though I am broken,
my left hand fingers still snap
as I find new ways to play on.

Digital Signals

As my disease progresses
little things become impossible.
My right hand is rebellious.
It grows weak with passing time,
foreshadowing my fading future.
My fingers are luckless.
Lazy middle finger won't cross
its dear digit brother index
to bring me some sign of luck.
Together they have curled to fight,
unable to make the peace sign.
They must act as individual agents.
One taps message keys here.
The other stretches not straight
but stands up as tall as it can
to tell this disease, "Fuck you!"

How to Boil a Frog

Don't place me in boiling water; I will
jump out lickety-split.
Warm, clear water is the way to fool
me - seduce me.
I am too dumb to sense subtlety.
You experimented to satisfy curiosity,
while I lived among the lily pads,
a carnivore looking forward to my next
fly.
Touch me, cold blooded, like your
murderous plan.

You capture me and I humor you.

I sense sultriness, but underestimate
the slow boil.
You have no darting tongue, so you
are cunning.
You lull me to sleep with the warmth
of this copper pond.
Breezy evaporation eases me toward
death.
Deep inside my anuran brain, I warm
to sleep.
Unable to escape among violent
bubbles, I dream in green:
dead frog swimming, hopping, hoping
for my final meal of dragonflies
breathing fire.

Slow Electrocution

Stray impulses jolt relaxing muscles.
Why is my body ruled by electricity?
My neurons play a video game
pulsing here, zapping there, ever
buzzing.
I am no longer O Captain, my
Captain.
I am controlled, ruled by an alien force
and it is not a force that is with me
but devastatingly against me.
Not that this fearful trip is close to
done,
not that there was ever rhyme or
reason
to this herky-jerky dancing of mine
but at least there was some
semblance
of what I thought was universal
power.
Now, I am Flash Gordon,
tortured at the cruel discretion
of Merciless Ming on Mongo
sitting in his Emperor chair
meeting out evil punishment
crossing my wires and shorting out
my once trusty electrical system.

Hand Me Down

We are the stream of humanity
passing life from hand to hand.
We are the bucket brigade
working tirelessly, steadily
against flame lapping tongues
like a herd of milk thirsty cats
at our unsuspecting sad souls.
Feverishly prime the pump,
fill the bucket and pass it quickly on.
Empties coming swiftly back
are as important as the refills.
Our dead silently fall away.
Fill in the gaps and reach!
There are fillers born per second,
let them join in and move down
as we grow taller, denser, older
becoming more feverish every day.
Atmosphere thickens with smoke
but the human heart is resilient.
When the inferno is overwhelming
reach for the alarm bell
call for reinforcements
to spell the bucket brigade.

Ruminating

Pacific breeze awakens us,
curled up by a blazing fire.
Not everything can escape
up past chimney bricks.

Something remains in our room.
It holds us ever together,
knowing that love is formed
from delicate intimacy stone.

In each mind · the same thought:
that we were made for each other,
fashioned from the same block,
carved marble of two as one.

Manhattan Island living now,
mixing, sharing the warmth
of flameless electric embers
finally alone together, ruminating.

Circus Lifer

The circus is my life.
I was the daring man
on the flying trapeze,
never working without a net.
Then I walked the tightrope
and after a damaging fall
I cleaned up after elephants,
wearing painted clown tears.
Fully recovered from internal injuries,
cracking the distracting whip,
fending with the attracting chair,
I put my head in the lion's mouth,
making sure it was well fed first.
I became shaky handed prey,
slipping into this sideshow
from my center ring spotlight.
I went from being the strong man
bending steel bars bare handed
to being relegated to the freak wagon
where I waste away before the eyes
of the young and the old,
like Kafka's sad hunger artist.
"Step right up folks,
See doctors make a pincushion
of a once high flying daredevil."

Wire Walk

Cable up and make it tight
thick as a childhood sidewalk crack
clamp barefoot toes down
while arms balance the wire walk.
Gravity is an uneasy lover.
Falling will define a hard landing
32 feet per second squared
and squared again and again
until falling at the speed of sound
turns into a heavy light year.
Just this side of paradise
the dear doctor gives me pills
that will add 10% to my life.
I seek quantification in months
from an aging accountant
adding up my debts of sin
on an inaccurate abacus
measuring thirteen month years.
My hands are helpless
to reach into coat or pants pockets
to search for ways to pay that debt.
I look up for a layaway plan.
My past precious earthly possessions
hang like a smelly pair of old sneakers
dangling by dirty shoe laces
up on a sagging telephone wire.

Mid Bridge

I stop mid GW Bridge
staring down old Hank Hudson's
River.
They actually jump from here?
After judging the height
my eyes are drawn away.
I spy my city in the daylight
etched against a perfect blue sky.
So much of what I was,
what I am lives there.
A Tugboat driven barge pushes north.
It will pass under my feet
never noticing I existed
amid the rushing stream
of big rigs and commuters
midway between my NJ birthplace
and the NYC place I now call home.
I look out on both life ends.
I see the tugboat is named *Comet*.
I wonder if there is an air bag aboard
to catch me if I should jump.
There is someone out on deck.
He waves and I wave back
with just enough humanity
to propel me back to life
and to my Manhattan home.

Eyes Open

Eyelids rise like fleshy curtains.
There is a dog barking next door.
My morning note to self,
"Don't stretch the spasms awake."
What dreams came last night
amid the jungle jumble of sleep?
REM slips me back under.
Men riding headless horses
chase me past Joshua trees.
At the edge I jump without a chute
hoping the terra cotta canyon floor
is a sea of stacked mattresses.
I wake with a start, still dreaming,
sleep walking in Riverside Park
eyes closed, footsteps automatic,
the scent familiar as mowed grass.
A falling leaf skims my sick hand,
future damaged legs stumbling.
Why am I always falling headlong
in and out of sleep, looking hard
for a sidewalk crack cause?
Swinging in and out of love sickness,
I search for the hidden code
of fair beauty's rhyme scheme,
the rhythm that makes me whole,
a balanced, fluid moving human biped.
Now two dogs are barking, signaling.

"There is a sick human next door."
"Sick humans are everywhere."
I rise, grateful for a new sunrise.

Joyous Sky

Looking up is not always easy
but even this gray overcast sky
sucking every single color out
of all things oxygenated, animated
brings me to a smiling place
where misery is defeated,
left to blow silently away,
like leaves picked up by hope
tickling my shoe bound toes
and finding my hiding funny bone.
Suddenly, I am laughing
at a tale told by this idiot,
full of my sound and my fury
whistling a snappy tune.
I become New York rhythm and blues,
dangerously dancing down Broadway.

Body Sand

On my right hand
under the shallow skin
of my right middle finger
on the side I can't see
there appears a tiny bump.
For months I scratch
the impenetrable skin
but once a year
irresistible itching comes
and out something appears,
a grain of hard crystal sand.
I swear, that is what it is,
a tiny grain of sand.
My good thumb picks it up
and transfers it to the index finger
and the digits play away
with something foreign, hard to
discard.
Every single year the process repeats.
They are lined up on my dresser
like sand soldiers reminding me of the
years.
But this time, just at this moment
I suddenly realize after over sixty
years
that I am nothing but an hour glass,
slowly, precisely, surely running out of
time.

90 Percent Man

I am still mostly operational
but the motor that runs me
has abandoned my right arm.
My fingers try to stretch out
as if I am poor Adam
up on the Sistine Chapel ceiling
reaching but not touching
the hand of perfection.
The weight of my cold fingers
leaves me desperately out of touch
as the sound of my misfiring motor
fills the heavenly cloud ether.
And now I am begging, pleading
for a divine hand-me-down,
a book of revised genetic code
that will reboot my hardening drive
before I become hopeless, helpless
depending, angrily, unwillingly
on the kindness of the same strangers
who knew a once strong, vital being.

Cut Flowers

My roots are rotting.
Cut me away from them
or rip me out like a weed.
Cut me with scissors
but follow safety rules
passed down to me:
never run with scissors,
hand sharp shears
with the point toward you.
Make my stalk bottoms sharp
and search high and low
for a crisp clean crystal vase
and a sunny window ledge.
Make sure to fill with water
from the fountain of youth,
or from the spring at Lourdes
which will sparkle in the sun.
Oh, and please don't forget
to add a packet of sustenance
fortified with love and caring.
Admire me now, day to day
as I live beyond my time.

Become Me

Go ahead and try me on,
my bouncy gait,
the one that remains
six decades on,
my receding hairline
devolves daily
like an ever ebbing tide.
My sad Irish eyes
betray what waits
deep in that cave
where you must retreat
to truly become my self.
There you will find me,
ever searching the darkness
now on a mission to aid you
in your on-site inquiry.
Look hard for the reigniting
main filament string glow
that brought on the bright ideas
of a youth looking forward to the
future.
Sit here and rest on my laurels
hearing me slowly, strongly reciting
the self-full words of this poem.

Concrete Shoes

Walking on water is hard enough.
Jesus made it look divinely easy
but he had help from heavenly Pop.
I hope for sharp stick immortality
while boldly, I carve my two initials
in driveway apron wet cement,
not realizing my feet are sinking
into custom made concrete shoes.
I walk avenue to avenue
like Riverside bound Frankenstein
hoping the bridge won't fail
before I reach the Hudson.
I foresee the fickle future
in my diving helmet emporium.
In a locker with my name on it
Davy Jones gasps for air,
laughing at the bottom of the river
waiting for a cement splash.
Sweet Jesus, I am bounding
across the deepening river waters
unsinking, unrelenting, undrowning.
I smile with the pebble circles
that grow wider and wider and wider
letting the people of the city know
that there's a new JC in town.

Key Me

Scratch your name on my forehead,
make it match my mind imprint.
Write it silver mirror backwards
so I can read it while shaving.

We are in every muscle memory
never lost in brain to nerve
translation.
All your electronic discharges
gather trapped on my tongue tip.

We are stammering now, convulsing,
screaming a facsimile of our name.
Our lips curve in a sardonic smile
that holds the best of what we were.

The inner impassioned voice is
deafening
as it shouts from our thought chamber
traveling instantaneously
From mind into body saying,
"Listen, they're playing our song."

Monetized

Who the hell came up with that word?
I hope to God it ain't in the Bible.
Jesus monetized loaves and fishes,
allowing the meek to inherit the stock
market.

The disciples occupy Wall Street.
St. Peter, my financial advisor,
saves me from investing in a future
filled with uncertainly and rapture.

Why did I invest so much time
perfecting a masturbation hand?
It seemed like a very sound idea
for an altar boy seeking blindness.

Who made me? God made me
commit impure actions on myself.
My life has always been a venial sin
waiting in a dark alley to lure me in.

I curse the darkening evil sky,
knowing the Almighty is at work.
I anticipate a loaf and fish bounty,
as I stand drenched by torrential rain.

Last Chosen

Playground pick-up game choosing is a
hierarchy
with a pointing to this one and then to
that one.
The captain's fingers become less
enthusiastic
as the pool of un-chosen dwindles,
leaving one undesirable player.
I imagined that *unwanted* was my
fate
predestined in my mother's womb
because superiority had never
appeared
on any of the colorful court cards
the gypsy caravan left behind for me
scattered face up and face down
like pages of the broken unbound book
about the failures of my young athletic
life.
Loneliness intensifies in team sports
when no teammate wants you
or ever thinks to direct the ball your
way.
But just before *loser* became my
brand,
when the game was on the line,
the captain fumbled the ball away
and some wayfarer spirit rolled it my
way

whispering, "The final shot is yours to take."
I grabbed the sphere as if it was my world,
took a desperate shot at becoming a *winner*
and that score put me among the chosen ones.

Agoraphobic

Self-shut-in
encloses himself
like a water-moated king.
Locking his mate out,
he may be shaken,
but won't be taken alive.
There is *a rat* in separate.
There is a lion in winter.
Yellowed newspaper pages
stuffed under the locked doorway
and in window casements
keep out the deadly draft
of overflowing human kindness.
He thanks God for the canned food,
his sorry hands can no longer open,
but there is no, "let me help you with
that"
or lightening bolts from above.
If only he could look and truly see
the sky is so beautifully broken,
the evergreen trees are just shadows.
There is no color now.
Light gray turns blacker
and the only present dangerous sound
is the arc of a short in the plaster wall.
He waits patiently for the fire

while singing, "My lonely life
is burning down, burning down,"
slightly, purposely off key.

Idle Thoughts

Disuse causes atrophy.
Where are the light bulbs
above the minds of youth?
Curiosity kills nothing
if there is guidance,
a reaching hand held out
on the train platform,
a warning from experience.
It is not knowing the answers
but rather fielding the questions,
remembering, recounting stumbles,
knowing what hunger brings
and when to stoke up the belly
furnace.
That is the feeding magic trick.
Abracadabra, poof goes the smoke
revealing a wonderland rabbit
who leads knowledge seekers on
down the terrifying black hole
to the cavernous inner mind
shinning like a diamond mine.

Bully

Go ahead, show off the fact that you
are better, smarter, prettier, taller,
thinner, tougher,
that I am worse, dumber, uglier,
smaller, fatter, weaker,
that your skin is clearer, lighter,
darker,
that my English ain't good,
along with anything else you can hurl
my way.
I wonder what motivates your hate,
your disregard for the feelings of
"other" humans
you spit upon, degrade, beat up with
fists, sticks, stones
and worse those razor sharp cutting
words;
you know the ones that your father,
mother, bothers, sisters,
your friends, enemies, classmates used
on you.
They hardened you, so hard that you
forgot
the horrible pain and humiliation they
inflicted
and instead of learning what bullying
does
you passed it on like an abused child

37

who grows up to become an abuser.
Please accept this flower,
it is a sign, a symbol of the beauty
of the soul that is within us all,
our brothers, sisters, friends, and even
enemies.
Many years on, when you think back
and you too have been beaten and
broken,
feeling guilty for what you did
to him and to her and to me
put your mind at ease, my friend.
For my part, I forgive you
because I became something in spite of
you
and just maybe, because of you.

Lemon Morning

It is a taste and a scent
of bittersweet lemon
starting in a dream factory,
continuing, eyelid splitting
just moments from the alarm
shaking the sunlit curtains.
This morning reaching is warmth-less
with no bedside other body,
no sleepy morning moan.
Cold sheets are dead.
Solitaire is lifelessness.
Turning mystery pillows over
like faceless playing cards
reveals no Tarot fate.
Coffee scent is welcome
leading barefoot padding
to a caring kitchen.
Waist surrounding arms
preserve renewed union.
Pushed into a wooden chair
straddled like a saddle broken steed
lovemaking begins a new day.

Trained Junkie

The monkey rides her
and she rides the train.
Those eyes are dope full.
I recognize the heroin nod
from friends dead and gone.
Somehow she got dressed
in platform boots, leather jacket,
and knee-holed jeans.
Almost respectable, fashionable,
she leans in for a close reading
of poet, Charles Bukowski,
who completes her downtroddeness.
That drunken fool scribbled
sparkling lowlife notes between
binges.
She is bent so low now
like a closing jackknife.
The tourist woman next to her
looks very uncomfortable
as old Chuck's book slips
falling to the dirty floor.
Junkie girl is unaware.
The downtown riders freeze.
The train tunnel halts
at my subway stop.
I pick up her book
and read the title,
hoping for a clue

as to why this young girl
has descended into hell.
Tales of Ordinary Madness
I tuck it snugly in her vice like elbow.
Our mutual conductor is amplified,
I hear his warning, she does not,
"Stand clear of the closing doors."
Just ahead of our stainless steel
separation
I hear Bukowski smack down again
in a desperate drunken stuper.

Train Fly

How the fuck did you get here
from foul Fourteenth Street air
down the filthy staircase
through the flipping turnstile
past homeland security
to join these subterranean tubers?

And how do you manage to fly
at exactly the same speed
as this uptown express?
Are your wings in sync
with the engineer driving
like a crazed maniac
through this tunnel of
infernal, eternal midnight?

And out of all the voyaging strangers
you find my damaged hand to rest
upon.
Somehow I hear you panting,
your thousands of eyes trained on me
as if you think I knew
poor fragile, sequestered
Emily Dickinson heard you buzz
when she gave up and died.

But little fly, you are unaware
that your secret takeoff strategy

is hidden deep in my brain
and as you take off backward,
my open good palm snares you
not to crush your tiny life
but to carry you out
from this human cemetery
past homeland security
through the flipping turnstile
up the filthy stair flights
to Christopher Columbus Circle.

All the while you buzzzzzzzzz
in my tingling, fleshy fly trap.
Now, with a slowly opening hand
I bid you a fond farewell
saying, "Fly on sweet angel."

Kind Lightning

Come for me here.
I wait on the platform
looking for your golden light
reflected on the tile wall
shining on the silver track.
Thank you for not striking
in the middle of my skull,
where the infant soft spot hardened
locking out easy enlightenment.
Thank you for electrifying the dust
surrounding my footprints
leaving the only evidence of me
for the aliens who are to come.
They will know of my fossil self.
I thought, therefore,
I imagined that I was.
The train pushed air stream
subverts my silly thoughts
of eventual immortality.
Please be a downtown local.
The express doesn't stop here.
Let your doors enfold me.
Bring me safe inside.
Start slowly, pick up speed.
Race me into your night.
Take me where you will.

Unfinished Romantics

Sand me down.
Start with rough grind
and move to finer, finest.
Take off my varnish,
now a yellowing patina.
I am a human antique
without the precious antiquity.
Take me back to live among
the 19th Century Romantics.
Put me in lock step
with Byron, Keats, Shelley.
Words worth me.
Place me in a corner
of Blake's secret garden
where I can hide undetected,
while the crazy bastard
dances around nude,
struggling to differentiate
innocence from experience,
as I struggle
to write this poem
on a falling leaf
during a hurricane.

In and Out of Dreaming

When you wake I will be there
as we exit your dream together.
The life and death that separates us
will disappear like smoke.
We will be caressing, kissing,
pushing our breath out
and when we release,
our lungs will fill to the brim
with the scent of flowers
and our ears will fill
with the sound of waves
as the ocean speaks
telling us that we are safe
alone together, at peace
with each other.
And then it will begin,
the exploration of passion,
and we will moan
as we reenter an eternal dream
that will dare not touch reality.

Rushing to Wait

We are moving in real time.
Anxiety captures me here
as young students discuss
what it means to be right handed.
No, seriously they do
as I stare at my hand damage.
Yes, it is right that is wrong.
The visit to the ALS man
will confirm that fact
unless a miracle occurs.
Passing Harlem housing projects
I feel so very fortunate.
I am trapped between two crazy men
one at each end of the subway car.
168th street stop saves my ass.
Columbia Medical overshadows
this sunny cold afternoon.
I settle into the waiting room.
I hate being among the infirmed.
Didn't used to feel that way,
but I am sick now, like they are,
up on the steely razor's edge
with pessimism on one side
and optimism on the other.
The question is whether
to fall with a smile or a frown.
Waiting for my name to be called,
the physical world seems to disappear

leaving me looking for an exit.
I hear my formal, saintly name
echoing
as if down my grammar school
hallway
from a rosary wielding Dominican
nun.
"Joseph? Joseph!"
Obediently, I rise to face my fate.

All Kindling Aside

My father taught me
paper lights the kindling
kindling lights the logs.
There is love in familiarity.
There is joy in a sunrise
and in an initial embrace
as life finds its serpentine way.
I slither through decade flashes
of a life well and unwell lived.
No one, and I mean no one
gets out even partially alive.
Look at the statistics closely:
There are 322,762,018 in this country
and only 30,000 of them have ALS.
That makes me a very rare American.
I tell the self-pitying echo in my head:
Never you mind; just fucking feel.
Open those stuffed up receptors.
Put a spring in your step
and one life marching foot forward.
Allow tiny bits of joy to thrive.
Never you mind that disheartening
thought.
It is just a dreary home invader,
searching with flashlight in hand
for your most valuable possessions:
breath, vitality and a bit more
precious time.

Even if the destructive intruder
asks if you are feeling cold
say, "Yes," strike a match and relight
your fire.

Trip

My wife says, "Let's haul ass."
The train is coming.
I trip on the stairway
just as I might have tripped
a carefree year ago,
before the dreaded diagnosis.
It is different now.
It may be a sign
of coordination deterioration.
I am okay, unhurt, unscathed,
yet concern surrounds me
like a black veil.
I am up and walking.
We have missed the train.
Becky smiles holding up two fingers,
our signal for next train in two
minutes.

Borrowed Blue

Velvet blue-sky lies
like a caught child
unwilling to admit
that the day is frigid.
Baiting those who venture
to choose thin material,
for hold off winter protection.
Unseasonably warm
rolls off the tongue
like a child's runaway sled
cutting wet melting snow
and then free-falling
through the bone yard
of trees stripped naked.
Just like winnowing me
they stand desperately in need
of a leafy flowery coat
to battle this frosty morning.

Damn Amsterdam

There is something here,
it is a loss of light
when I go elsewhere
floating upward
and finding reality
to be that lonely place.
Flesh greets concrete
as my numb hand heel
is skinned and bleeds.
I press it down to ascend
letting my fiery pulse
find its weary way
down into the beat
of this vibrating island.
And somehow,
this Irish Catholic boy
on Amsterdam Avenue
allows mind and body
to create a language.
Two voices echoing
inside this bony skull
wordlessly communicating,
crying, shuttering;
tears streaming down
cheeks baptized
with sad moments.
The traffic flow stops.

The salty mixture returns
following recent tracks.

No idea why
I am left here
at the crossroads between
the Western Lands
and the land of the living
where cement sidewalks battle
with white lined blacktop streets.
Like un-waving surf,
and un-absorbing sand
today, they align together
in the sunshine,
in the bitter cold,
that comes between
my waning pleasure
and my waxing anxiety.

"The world dies with the individual."
· Nabokov ·

Where Goes Knowledge?

Knowledge is power, yet it has no control
over the grim reaper, no life ending
lengthening.
Where goes the knowledge and the
appreciation of beauty?
The stuff gathered in the brain over a
lifetime of learning.
I imagine a movie scene:
a man intends suicide at the end of the
day.
He sits silently turning pages,
intensely studying a book.
Why?
The content goes in but then, when he
dies,
when his brain decomposes, has that
meticulously sought
world of beauty, art and literature
been studied all for naught?
Perhaps there is a brilliant place, an
undiscovered country

that is filled to the brim with leftover
intelligence bits
from the convoluted brains of the
dearly departed,
who gathered it all up during their
now ended lifetimes.
And in that beautiful country
I want to swim the waters
of their deep grey matter memories,
soaking up their hard earned learning,
body-surfing the thunderous waves
that crash on the sparkling sandy
shore
of the Sea of Collective Consciousness.

Life in Reverse

Dreams bring on the freedom to dance.
Waking brings increasing limitations.
Progressing de-nerving has me
devolving,
in reverse gear undoing growing
pains.
Sometimes I laugh at my ineptitude
unable to accomplish the simple
things
zipping, buttoning, gripping, holding.
There is hope in finding new habits
and joy in remembering the old ones.
My grandfather taught me to sign my
name.
My mother taught me to tie my shoes.
My father taught me to throw a
knuckle ball.
Skills gone like a seeded lawn under
spring snow.
I imagine traveling back to innocence,
ignoring the strangling bracelets of
thorns.
Even now, I find new roses blooming,
brightening my once traveled return
path.
As precious as muscle memory may be
other learning is not ruled by nerve
fibers.

I will spark the remaining fuel of the
fire within
using any communication method
possible
to file reports from the battlefield
front.
No matter how much my shell
deteriorates
both wide-eyed innocence and
experience
will surround me like night bloom.
Look for me in your rearview mirror
as I live the rest of my life in reverse.

Medical Trial

There are white blood cells
from thousands of humans
running like Pamplona bulls
through my blood stream.
They are my army in armor,
fighting the good fight
to save me from rebel neurons.
Nurse Karen is their general
and she injects the troops in
through a tiny steel tunnel.
Drip by drip by drip
their Fantastic Voyage commences.
I root for my white army
struggling to D-day a beach head,
where hooded death contemplates
his black checkmate move.
All but lost on this alien shore,
I hear only the pebbles moving
in the pounding surf
as I am saved by a tidal wave
spilling chess pieces everywhere.
Frustrated Death struggles to open
a soggy, disintegrating Seventh Seal.
I push away, swimming out,
while being buoyed by another day.

Note before the wedding poem:
The depression of a life-threatening
disease is like grief; it can only sustain
itself for so long. Like an Irish wake,
which begins with quiet sadness and
tears but soon becomes a loud,
laughing celebration of a life; the
beautiful distraction of one of life's
joyful events breaks down depression's
dark door to let the sun shine in. I
wrote this poem for the New York
Central Park wedding of my amazing
son, JT Curtis and his lovely bride,
Hiroe Sato.

Love Defined

Defining love is not easy
For thousands of years
Poets have tried again and again
To express the true meaning of love
Shakespeare wrote in *Love's Labour's Lost*
"When love speaks, the voice of all the gods
makes heaven drowsy with the harmony."

Philosophers looked deeper
Trying to define love's nature
But the deeper they dug
The more mystery unfolded
Aristotle studied the emotion and said

"Love is composed of a single soul
inhabiting two bodies."
Ambrose Bierce defined the noun love
as
"A temporary insanity, curable by
marriage."
You see Love is a riddle
Wrapped in a mystery
Deep inside an enigma
Where heart shaped puzzle pieces
Rarely fit tightly together

But a man raised in the far west
And a woman from the Far East
Found each other against the odds
Amid the madding crowd
That is New York City.

Like a new day's sun and the horizon
line
Two unique cultures were bound
together
While the gods provided a dazzling
dawn
That was reflected in Central Park
Lake.

Listen now and you will hear their
vows
The sincerely said sound of "I will"
Spoken in English and Japanese
As echo angels continue to carry the
words
Through the air that surrounds us.

Take note, ye poets and philosophers

Whether used as a noun or verb
Love's true definition
Exists right here, right now
In the essence of two lovers
Two now happily married people
Hiroe Sato and JT Curtis.

*For my beautiful wife Becky on our
35th Wedding Anniversary.*

35 Years On (to be exact)

They were married
In The Little Chapel
On a San Diego day
Mid-October (to be exact)
They lived year to year
In more apartments
Than they can count.

Four years in, they had a baby
A beautiful son (to be exact)
Raised in the California sun
While she taught college
And he wrote for TV
They made a living
And watched him grow.

Ten years flew by
They sometimes lost their way
He did (to be exact)
But she stuck by him
And they sheltered in place.

Their twentieth anniversary yielded

A dark emotional storm
And when his mind split in two
She grabbed him
By his shoulders (to be exact)
And shook him awake.

A twenty-fifth anniversary
Brought an economic storm
When their home dream collapsed
So they packed it, not in
But up (to be exact)
And they joined their son in NYC.

And 34 years on
An electrical storm begins
To ravage his twitching body
And she sticks with him
By him (to be exact)
He falls and she picks him up
As always, (to be exact).

On this 35th anniversary
They hold each other's hands
Tightly (to be exact)
She says, "I don't need a card.
I don't need flowers
Just write me something."
So here it is my dear, Becky:
"35 years on, I am still mad about
you."
We love each other (to be exact).

Loss is Gain

Departure is like arrival
Just in reverse motion
With a discovered country
Tucked in my memory valise
I try to concentrate
On those things I did
Rather than those things
I could have accomplished
If only I had worked harder
Nosed up to the grindstone
Not to the devil's playground
Remembering my never dreamed of
That is where I smile
At the thought back then
Of my tiny expectations
When my imaginings
Were so limited in scope
And the circle around me
Was so comfortably closed
But there was a gate
There is always a gate
Once found, it leads
To other gates unseen
Opening, revealing to me
Inviting me to pass through
Bringing the dual joys
Of curiosity and learning
To my unquiet mind

Pushing open perception's door
Always looking for more.

Slurred Speech

Tongue-tied, I bite down
Wincing in bloody pain
Third time this month
My teeth have attacked
Trying to eat me up
One bite at a time.

My tongue is unruly
But then again
It always has been
Venturing out of bounds
I try to rest it
But I am an Irishman
And storytelling is my life.

I am running out of time
Now I am asked to record
The sound of my voice
1,600 words and phrases
So that when I can't speak

My synthesized words
Can help broadcast
My thought and ideas
Forming the voiceover
To the stalling, slowing story
Of the rest of my life.

The Verb To Be

Go ahead, Jay,
And just be
Forget the rules
You are alive
God damn it
You move
You breathe
You eat
You think
The future is not yours
To either define or see
It never was
Sit on the living bench
Collecting life's splinters
You are nowhere near
The eternal dirt bath
Summon up the strength
To ignore medical fate
And embrace hope
Remember the old joke:
The doctor gave him
Six months to live
He couldn't pay his bill
So the doctor gave him another six
months.

Farewell Tour

Traveling coast to coast
To my California homes
The long goodbye shortens.

My life was evenly spent
Flirting with two oceans
Meeting my wife by one
Having a son by another.

Good friends in LA
Remember CBS TV City days
There are no tears here
Promises are made
Into a future I may not have
"See you in New York City."

We drive to San Diego
Older friends throw a party
Becky smiles at me
As I hold court, a dying king
Recounting my star daze.

We stay right on the beach
Where the surf and sand
Fight for command
Entertaining my eyes
Waiting with me patiently
For our glorious sunset.

Moonlit Sunrise

There is a daily dissolve
Between dark and light
Between heaven and hell
Hovering like a hopeful lover
There is a razor sharp edge
That is stretched out
A ghostly horizon line
Being painted only for me
With vanishing point perspective.

I imagine a day in the forest
Dawning with Jesus rays
I bring it into sharp focus
To see its subtle glow
It is my solitary mind view
The sound fades up slowly
Of waking fowl and insect prey
Just as a dead tree falls.

I swear there is sound here
Even if I am the only
Pictured sound witness
A laughing sound follows
And turning, I discover
A sole shining silver smile
Willing like no other
To verify all I see and hear.

Lastly

My last poem is wordless
It is the scent of April bloom
A slap and a baby cry
The pad of first steps
The turning of pages
Crayons coloring a book
Pencil scratching a name
Over and over again
Playmates having fun
"One 'o cat" game in the street
The smell of fresh rain
The silence of a snowfall
Heart pounding at first love
Emptiness of lungs
When love is suddenly gone
With song after song
Folk rock 'n roll blues jazz
Church bells ringing
And a new baby crying
A world spinning by
The sound of a smile.

And then:
Blood filling tubes
Over and over again
Loud bangs in an MRI
Screeching of muscle tests
Gulp of pills going down

And the struggling sounds
Of just trying to get dressed.

Now there is only
The gentle breeze
As my memory climbs
Step after step until
Reaching your sleeping ears
This poem takes form
Somewhere in your dream.

www.ingramcontent.com/pod-product-compliance
Lightning Source LLC
Chambersburg PA
CBHW060555100426
42742CB00013B/2566

* 9 7 8 0 9 9 8 6 0 6 0 1 9 *